AF424461

Gumbo Bottoms Pure Pot Still Poets Society Presents:

Homebrew

Edited by Jon Freeland,
Ken Gierke and Jason Ryberg

OAC Press
Belle, Missouri

Acknowledgments:

The authors would like to thank the editors of the following publications where some of these poems (in one form or another) were formerly published:

Walter Bargen: "How we learn to fly:" *LatinosUSA,* "In Order to Survive:" *MasticadoresCanada*

Ken Gierke: "Tapestry:" *The Short of It,* "Embers to Stars:" *Poetry Breakfast,* "One True Constant:" *Formidable Woman Sanctuary,* "In Stillness:" *Heron Spirit* (Spartan Press), "Driving Back to a Love Supreme:" *Literary Revelations*

Barbara Harris Leonhard: "Our House of Hungers:" *Three-Penny Memories: A Poetic Memoir* (Experiments in Fiction, 2022)

Mark Pottorff: "Mom:" *Around That Old Table* (Spartan Press, 2026)

Richard Stimac: "Waynesville:" *Museum of Americana* (2025)

Agnes Vojta: "Flotsam," "Vineyard in Dresden," "Rewired:" *As It Ought to Be Magazine,* "The One who Left:" *Bindweed,* "Naming:" *Young Ravens Literary Review,* "The Yew Trees with their Bitter Berries:" *Made of Rust and Glass,* "We Call it Gravity," "To Call this Place Home," "A Fractal of Generations:" *Love Song to Gravity,* (Stubborn Mule Press, 2025)

Clarence Wolfshohl: "Spring Blooms:" *Ilya's Honey* (Summer 2015), "The Wisteria:" *Dragon Poet Review* (February 2018), "Wolf Tree:" *Versewright* (online), "Fishing at Lake of the Ozarks:" *All roads lead to home* (September 2016), "The Ghosts of Toledo:" *San Pedro River Review* (Fall 2017), "Clay:" *New Letters* (85.1)

Table of Contents:

Ken Gierke

Janelle Harris

Melinda Hemmelgarn

Introduction:

Gumbo Bottoms is a tiny bar in the heart of the City of Jefferson in the great state of Missouri. It's an alley with a lid on it; we love local, regional, craft everything.

Homebrew, as a definition. means made at home, rather than a store or a factory. That's pretty open-ended and I believe sums up this poetry club. The skill levels of this club range from super novice, like myself, to accredited, published, and respected writers.

I was told once that the great skill set in writing is learning the rules, then learning how to break them. It's fitting that people who hang out at a tiny bar known for rotating craft beer, craft whiskey, and craft roots music, would be the breeding ground for craft words. Homebrew is that craft, learning the rules in order to have the right to break them, push the envelope.

This group constantly inspires, supports, engages, enriches, and normalizes art, no matter how strange. With great pleasure we present our latest offering to the gods of grace and karma and love.

A special thank you to the Osage Arts Council - an amazing group of humans involved with promoting and protecting all kinds of art from mid-MO and way beyond.

Earnestly good humans. Thank you for the love and support, and that's from everyone involved in the club.

So, here is the sophomore effort of a poetry collection from us to you. Gumbo Bottoms Single Pot Still Poets Society proudly presents:

Homebrew!

When in doubt, do it yourself,
push the envelope, be weird….

Slainte,
Padrigh Stiofan

-Stephen Erangay, Owner Gumbo Bottoms Alehaus

A Second Home

Gumbo Bottoms Alehaus has been home to The Gumbo Bottoms Single Pot Still Poets Society since late 2019. Its core members have found it to be a place of inspiration, from the ever-changing art that hangs from its walls to the words of fellow poets. It's a place where writers can voice their concern over the state of current affairs and bare their souls through words about love, loss, and identity, knowing their statements will be met with acceptance.

And yet, this poetry collective is more than its core members. It holds the voices of poets who travel 30 miles, 130 miles, and even from across the country to share in the warmth and acceptance one would expect to find in a second home. As for those core members, they welcome with open arms those who visit Gumbo Bottoms, whether new to them or easily recognized, eager to hear those traveling poets and share their home with them.

Homebrew is an extension of that home. It holds the voices of those core members, as well as some of those who have traveled to be with them.

in a small-town bar

a man walks in a stranger

walks out a poet

-Ken Gierke

Homebrew

Keely Alexander

Love Letter to My Home

Home,

You never had a permanent address with me always
packing boxes, learning new streets, new schools, new
bedrooms where the walls didn't yet know my name

You never had a permanent address, instead you had
two names–Papaw and Grandma…Oh how my body
softens in your presence

The only spot on the map where my nervous system
stops holding its breath

Home is breathing deeply listening to Papaw's stories at
the kitchen table, his voice steady as a soft rain turning
chaos into something with a beginning, middle, and end

Home is breathing deeply eating flapjacks with
butterscotch chips, syrup pooling at the edges like a
small, sweet shore I could always return to

Home is breathing deeply playing in Grandma's closet
swimming in her clothes and jewelry learning softer
ways to be a woman than versions I saw elsewhere

1

Every visit home was a life jacket
coming up for air, thirsty to fill my lungs with love
something heavy in myself gently setting itself
    down for awhile

Papaw, an honored Vietnam veteran, you wrote
    poems of flashbacks
lying under dark clouds, unsure if you were dying
sounds of suffering blasting around you
until a small voice calls out "Papaw Donnie, come
    here, Papaw Donnie"
You wrote poems of this small voice pulling you
    back to life in the here and now

A young child intimate with storms inside my house
there were nights my own thoughts crept too close
    to a cliff's edge
I didn't always know what I was drowning in
only that I was exhausted from treading water

Then there'd be a phone call, a visit, a drive to your
    front door
each time your own voices pulling me out of something
that surely could have swallowed a
    young girl whole

You used to say, "you can't stop the clock" and
    you're right
time marched forward whether we were ready or not
but in your presence time slowed down enough
    for healing to sink in

You couldn't stop the clock, but you gave me hours,
    days, weeks
that were gentle enough to counterbalance the years
    that weren't

Now I'm the little girl grown up sitting across from
    patients whose pain
sometimes feels familiar, and I see the invisible
    architecture that held my life together

I had you

I had steadiness in a life that would not sit still

So many bedrooms, so many streets, a childhood that
    feels like a flipbook of front doors

I close my eyes and ask, what "home" really is?

I don't see a house, rather it's what I sense

I see Grandma at the stove asking me about my days
    like the answers matter

I see Papaw at the table, laugh lines deepening as he
listens pausing long enough between words for my
    nervous system to rest

I hear sounds of your voices in the next room

I taste coffee and smell something baking

I feel my shoulders drop the second I sit on your
      couch

My five senses mixing together with the deep knowing
that if I tell you my truth, you will still kiss my cheek
      goodnight

If I have made anything good of this life
if I help people
if I love deeply
if I choose healing
…it is because you first paved a path

Everything good I will do carries a trace of you, two
people who without ever saying the words taught a
young girl she was worth being kept afloat

We can't stop the clock, but you stopped me from
      being lost inside it

When I say I'm going home, what I mean to say is
I am going back to the love you share with me

And that love has never once moved

Walter Bargen

How we learn to fly

Featherless. Not an ounce
Of air in these bones,
Dense with marrow
And the traffic of blood.
Calcium solid. Two legs,
Thick-thighed, heavy-calved,
Over-boned knees,
Broad flat feet, nails not claws.
Two arms and a fervid desire
To perch on window sills
On the eighty-eighth floor,
If only for a smokeless breath,
A respite from the sudden fermentation
Of fuel, the culture of heat.
Dante circling the bubbling steel.
Nothing that resembles
light horny epidermal outgrowths:
The quill, the vane, the barb, barbule,
Barbicel, hamulus, needed to flutter
To the eighty-ninth, ninetieth floors,
And out over the cloudy river waters.
A few feathery steps,
A jump into the fire of flight,
Suit, blouse, billowing plumage,
Arms feathering the air,
Flamed by falling floors.

In Order to Survive

Under Piazza Euclid, under the cobblestones
and raw earth dug up for founding another Roman
    parking garage,
from too far back in some dimly lit, curtain-shrouded
back room, dark alley, far field, and crumbling time,
come thumbprints from the lead-encased boxes
of wax and flour-molded dolls.
Police forensics identify them as a woman's,
a witches' magic cast again.
From Apuleius' *Metamorphoses* comes clear
the deadly apparatus: spices, unintelligible metal
plaques, remains of ill-omened birds,
skulls savaged by wild beasts, spike-covered
noses and fingers, and charms cast over pulsating
viscera amid shrouds of incense.
Ovid worried over secretly skewered livers
affecting his love life. Hidden in the house's floors
and walls, Tacitus tells us of human body parts,
incantations, lead tablets engraved with Germanicus,
grandson of Augustus, heir of Tiberius,
who died of the *curses that bind tight*. How could
Victoricus the charioteer ever win
the Carthage race if his horses' legs
were bound, their eyes blinded, their soul
and heart so twisted they couldn't breathe,
and the same spells for the charioteers.

Yet the once-hidden, buried, nailed-down curse
pulled out of sand survives, as the winner did not.
Where are the witches, the diviners,
the soothsayers, to cast unintelligible
spells, to bind us so tight to peace
that each time a president moves
to take aim, we moan, we writhe,
we are seized, until the whole nation
swoons and forgets to listen.

John Clayton

Mama's Biscuits

Mama made biscuits 3 times a day
It was like breathing for her.
She started every morning this way.
Put the ingredients in a bowl and give it a stir.

There was no biscuit board.
Sift on some flour and turn the dough onto the table.
Don't work it too much.
That will make them tough.

That old sifter has some holes in the screen.
Turn the handle and the flour sifts out.
Around 20 thousand pans of biscuits that sifter
    has seen.
Those biscuits were good, about that there's no
    doubt.

The biscuit pan has a few dents.
That came from years of use.
Can't buy a new one, have to save a few cents.
On top of the biscuits smear some bacon juice.

Pop them into the old wood stove.
Splitting cook wood is a pain in the ass.
It has to be oak from the back 40 grove.

It has to be oak, so it will last.

She helped us practice our times tables and spelling
    words, too,
As she fried the sausage and egg.
Making the gravy was muscle memory too.
It takes a lot to fill a growing boy's leg.

The oven door opens and the biscuits come out.
It floods the room, with that delicious smell.
Thinking about it I'm having a drooling bout.
Mama's biscuits are a memory as deep as a well.

Mother Had a Hobo Soul

My mother had a hobo soul.
Her hearth was open to hobos when it was cold.
She fed them all
both man and beast.
She didn't seem to mind in the least.
We were poor, in the extreme,
but I don't think I knew that.
I didn't understand the concept of greed.
It was simple, you share what you have with others
    in need.
You do that even when what you got
Ain't too much for you, just cut it in half so that
    there is two.
They say the hobos left signs on where to go.
For a handout, it was an X within an O.
Mama didn't know, of that I'm pretty sure.
She was always smiling when she answered the door.
Children learn from the examples they see.
I'm entirely convinced that's what happened to me.

Home Brew

His name was Otto Beardsley. Pronounced OTT TOE.
He was a share cropper in Ballard County, Kentucky
just outside of Wickliffe. After WW II he bought the
farm he had worked on the shares for years.

Ott Toe was my maternal grandfather.
You have probably guessed he was of German descent
and he liked to drink beer. Mama said he worked hard
but loved alcohol and gambling more than he did his
family. That has the ring of truth.

Two 53 gallon oak barrels sat at the corners of his back
porch. A down spout ran from the gutter to each of the
rain water barrels.

One of the barrels held rainwater. The other barrel,
well, it did hold a liquid but it was not rain water.

Ott Toe was an enterprising man who did not pass up
the opportunity to make a dime. Burley tobacco was
his main cash crop before the gov-ment got involved in
tobacco farming. What business does a politician have
telling a man how much tobacco he can grow. He also
grew a truck patch and in season that back porch looked
like a farmer's market. It operated on the honor plan.
There was an Old Judge Coffee can were the customer
made change and paid for purchases.

Some customers only came after dark and brought
their own containers. Most brought a 1/2 gallon jar
but some brought a gallon jug with the finger loop on
the neck. Those customers knew to slide the wooden
box with the hominy corn over to expose the spout
on the barrel that did not hold rainwater. I always
figured the Sheriff drank for free because Ott Toe
was never arrested for plying his trade.

I don't know when the home brew business started or
when it ended. I do know Ott Toe was still operating
in 1968 because I saw it with my own eyes and even
tried the product. I was on leave from the army. I had
gone to Heath to pick up a 20 ga. Frenchi from Uncle
Malcolm. I stopped by Ott Toe's house on my way
home. We sampled his home brew but it was not quite
ready so we went to Cairo and bought a 12 pack of
Falstaff. Ballard County was dry.

I drove him around in the Ohio River Bottoms while
we drank and he told stories. That was the last time I
saw him alive. I went to Vietnam in April and in the
Fall he shot himself. I hope his recipe did not die with
him. If there is an afterlife, I'm pretty sure Ott Toe
Beardsley is drinking beer, shooting craps and telling
lies.

Jon Freeland

Arcadence

(8.7.21)

In dark rooms,
there was no sunlight
like flashing pink, green, and blue
falling flat on crackled whitewash
and dingy gumshoe carpet.

What mysteries we created
and locked away beyond
yellow caution tape
and dying gates?

If I look hard enough
in wrecked angle space,
I swear I can see a bowl cut
dull in the clash of metal tokens,
tearing paper moments.

But nothing is there, plugged in
and wasting power,
a marching banned,
kicking and screaming to stay,
just like it always was.

Ears for Fears
    (8.5.24)

Shout.

A private game with public hopes,
only bitter therapy until you have
someone to share it with.

The best lines are drawn
in the paper, where they
can be crossed and dotted,
bold, underscored, undersold
separated from their parents,
given a Capri sun and a moonpie,
and left to crawl under the bleachers
after school to turn their backs
on Mother Nature, Huckleberry finished.

Let it all out.

When there's a chance I can a maze.
When violin means lead to violin endings.
When I despise myself, so sure you do too.
When it's a hug too loud, a wave too soft.
When it reminds me of Anthony Kiedis
and a Time-Life obsession with chant
and music you can juggle crystal sticks to.

When all our cannibals grew too old
to be fine and young.
When you have that thing only I can do.
When you don't know I can do it yet.
When it brings me peace,
but never contentment.

These are the things I can't live without.

Architects of a Moment

for Jude (12.23.21)

It was cinematic,
like bursting into
the reception hall at Nurragingy,
he approached me
with no reservations:
"we NEED to form a society!"

The bottoms kindling,
kindly conversation winding
scotch and the topography
of his voice, rolling in the east:
when we were done Keating,
I committed south, cloudy

spouting ideas. For all the hatred
of labels, titles are my favorite.
It had to be living.
It had to hurt like fathers.
It had to be tender,
the duty we have to we-other.
It had to be a new old,
start with a hold and end in a clap,
then ask for a hug?
It had to be parabolic,
launchpad learning to land
in a comfortable crash.

It didn't drive home,
instead coalescing slowly,
a cumul-Us attraction
of positive to negative,
heat connection, grounding
bitter invalidation.

What if our society
wasn't about striking
in the sense that bonds
are all-binding,
like approval and childly
fearing otherwise?

Ryan Letourneau mentioned
in passing people, not the main character,
who exist on a defining fringe of our lives:
"I'd like to think I played a role
in moving their story along, you know?
I was kinda like the architect of a moment."

And maybe there's no regret for less,
wishing for more, running from the unknown,
searching for the lost, swimming for beauty,
shouting for dignity, aching for answers,
lonely for duty, stranger for silence.

Maybe we choose to build
and keep it here.

Flying by the Seat of Someone Else's Pants
for Calli (4.1.24)

Flashes of a khaki office;
"I'm obligated, though I know you won't
listen, to recommend against it."

Today is a remnant, the denim of a younger,
thinner, less mechanical man.

"Do you think happiness
is intrinsic?"

She rolled back a bit, fluttering,
vibrating, titanium taurus toes
in a shared pool, extrapolating
on what can be felt
in an echo of an echo.

Can a stream of consciousness
have ripples, or by definition do
they require stillness?
My feet juggle arguments
while my hand became
a promise to moisturize,
to develop eyes for healing.

She enjoys asking, maybe more than
finding out. She's unsatisfied with my elbow

and I let her know we'll follow it, figure out
how the blow out goes. I wish it could be
now. Jason had just talked about
addictive personality and this is my
boundary exercise, being kind to myself with
the time I have to suffer looking at fallow follicular
    fields.

A woman walked in as the studio filled
with stars, houses, goddesses, grand designs,
    stubbornness, mentors,
constellations in creases and what they mean, and she
    edits what she wrote.
I don't even look twice at most of my poems,
but I stand rewritten, feeling solemn.

"What were we talking about?"

It was past, but in the map we became,
I moved on without worry about what
might be lost. I am practicing to keep
and question marks the spot.

Tattku

(3.4.24)

Body is given,
spiral-bound notebooks on legs;
Skin becomes language.

Scars are the promise
of vitamin see and you;
Survival bias.

Beyond the stopgap
medicine and surgery,
You're the one healing.

At least seven years
after hardest tissue forms,
it can still forgive,

Fortake or forsake?
Ink teaches that our leaves die
to feed what feeds us.

Hold roly polies
instead of role polizers.
Rejuvenautumn.

Then boldly question
"why moisturize the useless?"
Find your winter worth.

After allergies
subside and itchy few ours,
full eyes will agree:

They were your flowers
all along, what you became
inside out with love.

Back Words

(9.27.19)

Language is a storm seller in grief;
to be close, we have to lose.
To recover requires a cover.

He looked like Dad saying,
"Love is work in reverse."

Work is putting in the effort
until you finally get what you want.

Love is being lucky enough to have it already,
and keeping it until it's gone,

then struggling to deserve it.

I gasped for that Marlboro moment.
What if you strive for what you have, but don't own it?
What if it's not yours but you wish to be worth it?

"Do you think that may be a little harsh?"

How can you defend me?
I'm always going backwards.
Work in reverse is krow
and it's the only thing I eat
now that everyone opens
with, "are you ok?"

No. I talk too much
and my bring them back hurts.

"Maybe they never went to the basement.
Maybe they're still waiting for you upstairs,
calling because their love is your work
in reverse."

Ground Control

for Robin Freeland (9.27.19)

Sink or swim
doesn't work in space.
Still, you mastered the crawl,
all to float
broadcasting "am I in or off?
and which part is the deep end?"

It's too wet for new clothes,
quiet curses,
human pyramids,
leap frog,
red rover, red rover.

When they called you "martian,"
what was the words that could happen?

"Send Kicker right over."

Like late night lonely pots and pans
Like six months gone man
Like hot cocoa mix cockroaches
Like bomb threats from the next parking lot
Like sea salt bell buoys
Like the needle pointing home
Like Gregorian Chant Under the Bridge
Like Tot Fire Finder and D.A.R.E. to run away

Like Aerosmith alien invasion expeditions
Like abandoned, vanishing naked children
Like sneaking past the weak hallway floor spot
Like early morning defiant Knopfler in mist-covered
    mountains
Like tossing a closet full of shoes
so the now homeless mouse
migrates up Dad's sweatpants,
redefining "New Balance"

Do you think they were surprised
when they asked for war
and fucking GOT IT?

It's a dark matter,
but at mile 99,999
closing your helmet,
you spoke:

"You're the best poem I ever wrote."

And I'm feeling very still.

Risk of Rain

~ Alistair Freeland ~

When you see rain, what do you think?
Do you think of it as bad
weather or water from your sink?
When you go in the rain it makes you wet.
You would probably be annoyed,
sad, but don't fret.

Know that it's actually just
a nice shower on a nice day.
Where you sit in a rain
will be where you lay.

Whiskey Wanes

(7.7.25)

What I can give you:

Dust clouds roll across the screen
and I say he looks jovial.
You ask me what it means
To be gregarious.
You raise your eyebrow
and ask again.
Amicable.
You toss like grumbleweeds.
I look grinwards and hear Dad's voice
"GO GET THE DICTIONARY!"

You were born in the ashes
of its burning, so I could not give
you that battle cry. Instead, you got to
see what he always hid from me:

Anger
Damage
Erosion
Passion
Deconstruction
Talking about my feelings
as I struggle with my nobody else
wishing to give you culture,
connection and not my loud virus.

I inherited oceans, and seas, and rivers, and lakes, and
streams, and ponds, and whatever else you could fit
in a glass
and wash away people.
I can't help but curl; maybe I will
build enough muscle collecting
all I stare looms and beautiful whether
or knots quickly waking
grateful you're in my arms.

Climb the Maintain

(9.3.18)

You've grown so big and strong and tall. Remember
when you had trouble with this mountain? Now you've
conquered it and you're looking for the next. There'll
always be another, bigger you. Learn early what I'm
learning just now:

What you're doing is ok,
whether you go
an inch or a mile or stay,
keep that smile
for yourself almost always.

Then I'll look and know
though I struggled to show
you through my pain,
you're my favorite you
right now, and now
(and again, again, again)
that you (and I) have ever been.

Samara

(10.2.24)

Anemochory,
tight, uncertain lunar dance;
winded, you'll go far.

Ken Gierke

Tapestry

Fathers and brothers, sisters and mothers
Triumphs and trials, happiness and sorrow
Woven through tales past and those yet to finish
Blended with those of our children's children

A tapestry with folds that hold a fortune for those
Who understand the wealth of those tales, a texture
Felt in a moment of revelation with a child
An afternoon with a friend, a lifetime with a loved one

A brilliance in its deepest folds that inspires
In times of darkness or light, then and now
Woven as we come together to share that wealth
Ease the depth of that darkness, our compassion
Among the finest threads of life's tapestry

Embers to Stars

On a still night, flames rise
from crackling maple into thin smoke
that wafts upward in a loose spiral,
coaxed ever higher by glowing embers
that lie in the pockets between
those slowly settling logs. We sit
in a circle, feeling the warmth
seep into us, push against
the chill pressing into our backs.

Talk of the day's events behind us,
we gaze into the sky in awed silence,
a wordless communion blessed
by a blanket of stars, those flames
now as if nothing. Even as the fire
is reduced to embers, the night's chill
has no effect, for what could rival
a brilliance that inspires the imagination,
kindles wonder that knows no bounds
as it blazes across the sky?

One True Constant

Clouds part to reveal that same orb
viewed years and miles away, its shape
crisp in the cool October night air,
as we sat beside a fire talking about his youth,
mine, and that in store for my children,
knowing its light as the one true constant
throughout, as it is now, the miles no less,
for my grandchildren as they look to the night sky.

In Stillness

Where else would I want to be
than here, on quiet water?

The air, not so silent,
is filled with birdsong,

one chorus followed by another,
led by cardinals' call and response.

Louder and more insistent,
tufted titmice give voice.

A kingfisher passes by,
trilling out its lonely answer.

The only other sound
is the stroke of my paddle.

With stillness that holds such sounds,
where else would I want to be?

Momentary Permanence

I paddle and I paddle,
each stroke offering reward.

A bass, thrashing
in a futile struggle to escape
the grasp of an eagle
that swiftly rises from a river
in a slow January crawl.

The graceful nature
of a sycamore's white lines
against a blue March sky,
just as beautiful the full green
bloom of its leaves
in the coming months.

A dragonfly, the imperceptible
breeze of its lustrous wings
welcome in August heat
as it flits from a tree branch
to the bow of my kayak
to reeds that line the shore,
never still for long, until
it reaches the gray arm
of a tree rising from the river,
pausing to let me pass.

I drive and I drive,
each trip offering reward.

Children who greet me
with open arms, engage
in long talks of events
new and not-so-new,
as if they are one.

Conversations starting up
where they left off,
leaving off where they
are bound to start
once again. And again.

A granddaughter
who will read to me
the memorized tale
in her favorite book.
One who will walk with me,
a fast crawl more her speed
when last we were together.
Both milestones
in the passing years.

Places that never grow old,
never have when I was close
and never will,
even in my absence.

The sight of maple trees
when oak and hickory
have become my norm.
The blue of rivers,
waterfalls and lakes,
now that I'm surrounded
by muddy waters.

All of this welcome to me.
Permanent bonds, even
with their temporary nature,
like golden sycamore leaves
as they drift beside me, caught
in the swirl of my paddle,
as if to remind me
they will always be with me,
even if waiting inside graceful lines
against a blue November sky.

Modest Beginnings

Modest, even
by modest standards.
Not their first home,
but a starter after
a dozen years of rentals.
A stick home, really.
Thin walls and bedrooms
not much bigger than closets,
but their first true home
for another dozen years.
A place to start,
to improve, to tailor to
their needs. A place
where family came first
and friends were welcome.
And though every home
that followed offered more
amenities, within each
was found a warmth that came
from modest beginnings.

Labor of Love

Rushing to finish
concrete before it set
on a hot, dry August morning,

the drone of the cement mixer
laboring to turn out a single concrete pad.
Twelve feet by twenty,

a terrace on the side of the pavilion
we built the year before,
a place for family gatherings, reunions.

One more draw
for that long drive to visit
your home in the country,

to see you and hear the joy
and laughter of those gatherings.
Our last visit forty years in the past,

that pavilion still stands,
with different voices
and children in the home

that once was yours.
If I were to see it now, I know
I would hear the same laughter,

the faint ring of hammers,
the drone of that mixer, and
all the voices that made it a home.

Driving Back to a Love Supreme

Layer upon layer of clouds holding
a snow that never materialized
deliver a gray light,
but there's joyful anticipation at the start
of this long drive home like a pulse
of contentment. A love supreme.

Piano pulls me forward with resolve
when Coltrane comes in,
pursuing that love,
as drums urge me onward.

Like a psalm rolling through me,
clouds give way to blue sky,
the hint of home drawing me closer
on this long cold drive.

Janelle Harris

Oceans of Life

 Life comes at you in waves—
some gentle as your lover's whisper.
Some crashing, thunder-loud and wild.
Some so fast and violent, I lose my place
beneath their violent crash.

There are days I'm carried -
buoyant, laughing in the sun,
the salt-stinging - pure joy,
a moment that "takes my breath away",
the world shimmering, suspended,
each subtle splash a spark of wonder.

But some waves pull me under -
cold, relentless,
the water fighting for my oxygen
until I choke on silence,
and all I can think is
"I can't take a breath".

I learn - slowly –
to read the water's mood
to watch the horizon's hush and fury,
to brace before the swell,
to turn and swim with, not against,

to let go when I must,
to feel the rhythm,
to trust the rise and fall.

Between the fear and the awe,
I find my footing,
seeking the moments that lift me up -
when the spray, the sky,
the dizzying blue
remind me how it feels
to be breathless with joy,
not with dread.

So I keep watching the waves,
and I keep learning -
to dive, to float, to surface, to gasp,
to pull the air deep into my lungs.

Working for more. More days
when what takes my breath away
is not the weight of the world,
but the wonder of it.

Melinda Hemmelgarn

Bread is Love

If you follow your nose
down Parkhill Street
tucked in the heart of the city
you'll find a friendly red-brick house.

Stay with the scent
down the pebble path,
through the gate, and there
she stands.

A tall stone oven
birthing loaves of sacred bread
warm and golden, they
have risen to the occasion
of feeding a community.

Neighbors gather promptly
taste the bread, praise the baker
then wrap their loaves like babies
swaddled in cloth, to make their journey home.

On warm evenings, there is wine
and laughter, and catching up
and for a little while
the world is at peace
as we linger, connected by flour,
yeast, water and salt bread, hands, heart.

The Living Room

Come into my kitchen
can you smell the heady perfume?
It's late July.

Just home from the market
with armfuls of fragrance:
pungent basil melds with musky melons
fuzzy soft peaches, plump tomatoes
fruity scents swim with spicey notes
of ripe red peppers.

Spread out on the counter,
a seductive summer sampler
a bounty of intoxicants
a still life to behold.

Sacred nourishment
born from seeds
sprung from soil,
earth and water, sun and work
a farmer's freckled calloused hands.

I inhale, holding reverence
for abundance
olfaction
a hearty appetite
and the interconnected web
the beauty
of life.

Julianne King

chosen family.

chosen family is the language of the broken
the language of the children who have
pieced together nothings
into everything
the language of appetizers made into meals

chosen is life rafts sewn together
surviving the wakes of yachts
tearing through the water
mocking the unusual arrangement

chosen is the beauty
family is the hope,
that the choosers and sew-ers
will know the belonging
they have never known,
have always wished for

but family is no more certain than the water-borne
bonds Shakespeare warned us against
family can be unmade
alone more natural than interconnected
chosen more important than chanced
like comfort food
like Sunday mornings
like home

detention is such a gentle word for this torture.

His is the rib from which I was fashioned
we are only whole as one
as intended
as You
surely
intended
why then
are we tested
his was the Rib
from which i was fashioned
so give him back to me.
bring him home.

3 Heel Clicks

The reality of family separation and impossible choices.

2 a.m. is the easiest
waking up in his arms
babies sleeping down the hall
heartbeats synched
world righted

3 p.m. is golden
he's home from work
we eat
his hands coat mine
in warmth
in belonging

7 p.m. is chaotic. still.
babies fighting the sleep they need
mama all out of spoons
newness working against us all

9 p.m. is the hardest
echoes haunt me
the missing weight
teenage voices joking
shows unwatched
memories unmade
Tin man and Scarecrow
without Dorothy
without Toto

How did the wizard know
going Home
wouldn't kill them all

there is no word for what we are.

bert and ernie
sally and gilly
frances and jet
frog and toad
kite and anchor

what I'm saying is
we are a set
amputated
irrevocable
eternal

thicker than the water of birth
the blood of this covenant
beats steady in my
puppet heart

carter county.

there's a place where the pinetrees turn matchstick,
quiet has a texture like eardrums after concerts
and grasshopper knees are measurements
maple candies and fried okra flow like milk and honey
security blanket of stars
tin roof rainstorm aspirations
busted lip, bloody-knuckle conflict abated
know the deer and dirt and goony birds by name
sawmill sweet and lonely as she's ever been
flatland empty of everything but seeds and promises
strong and enduring as whiskey

trabajando.

sometimes
if i get high enough
and lay still enough
i can believe you are out of town
working

sometimes
i have you for a whole night
dream you for hours, eternities
and I wake expecting the heat of you
beside Me

it is always worse
punishment i am certain
because i have to remember all
over
again

but I keep sitting here
frozen
working on
welcoming the pain that meant
You
Were
Here.

New Home

fresh coatings of paint
announce what has always been
I create kingdoms.

Caitlin Korte

That Place

12.23.2025

A table in a random restaurant.
How are you?
What are you watching?
What are you reading?

Your mom did what now??

No need for the back story—
we already know.

Their presence,
a kind of medicine,
soothing to the soul.
A gentle salve against the
constant
onslaught of abrasions
that is
adulthood.

Hugs heavy with warmth,
depth and familiarity.
Laughter that spills over
turning into snorts.

There is
an unspeakable
comfort
in old friends.

A few precious moments
together
only a handful
of times a year.

Time loosens its grip.
And we return
if only briefly
to
that place.

The Mourning After

(for Heather) 11.19.2024

Does the sun rise
the mourning after your father dies?
(Asking for a friend)

I imagine not.
Between the weight of the rain
and the weight of his reign,
probably not.

There never was a son,
so why should there be sun today?
Only a daughter, a single daughter
held to the expectations and demands
of a world never built for her.
Yet she thrived.

Even in the rain, she will rise.
She will carry you,
she will carry all you built, forward.
Just like she always has,
even to your meticulous and obnoxious standards
through this dark
and into the oncoming reign.

An Ode to My Younger Self

08.12. 2025

Sweet child, where to start?
You have to wait.

It is awful, it is terrible.
Most things
    do not
     "get better."

Things will change.
Some will get lighter, you will get stronger.
But generally it stays the same.

Your body stays this shape.
I am so sorry.
The weight will drop some, but
the tummy roll, man ankles
giant calves and flabby arms
won't ever leave us.
You will get to learn an absurd amount
about women's Healthcare in America.

You wait 20 years, and you do
get to go to concerts and listen to the music you like
    the most.

You never learn to walk in heels,
you'll never be elegant or ladylike
in shape wear.

You do get to wear primarily black
and jeans and comfortable shoes.
There is more floral print involved
than you'll actually want, though.

The work is certainly not what we had in mind.
The relationships
are nothing you could comprehend.
But they are meaningful and as fulfilling as they can
be.

You get to borrow things, you get to pretend,
but most things are always
just beyond your grasp and understanding.
(Psssst - you've got the autism too)

You will always struggle - you will never be
    quite
    enough.

The sick sad truth is that - no one
and nothing is.

How Not to Eat My Family

Thanksgiving 2022

Oh boy, Thanksgiving
Cheers to a nice afternoon.
We totes got this fam.

Oh the dysfunction.
The undercooked, over cooked
not just the turkey.

Always the cleaning;
sinks, toilets, the floors and more,
old habits die hard.

Crispy on the top.
Mushy bits in the middle.
No one is amused.

Chosen family,
miss you so much more today.
Someday, we will all
be together for
these big meaningful events
held tight in my heart.

Waiting on uncle.
As per usus, he's running late.
You were told 2, sharp.

Every year, same
the dad is getting hangry.
Yearly traditions.

Oh baby brother,
still in bed at 1:30.
Wake up sweet baboo.
Jump in bed with you,
oh how the tables have turned.
My turn, to pounce you.

Dad made the turkey.
Hey, this is pretty tasty!
Is that possible?

Internal Tides

02.13.2023

We like the moon
cuz she is close to us.

Close to us, in all the ways
that make us human.

Pocked, scarred, barren
and yet
she knows her worth
at all times.

She takes pride
in every stage
of her phases.

I finally get to see
myself
and the moon,
through your eyes.

Staring down at me,
pulling at internal tides,
loving me,
like I love her;
regardless
of those internal tides.

Barbara Harris Leonhard

Our House of Hungers

I.

Dad, his own best friend.
Adventures on the sandy beach
of Lake Michigan, his playground
for swimming and skating.
Nature musters legends.

The winter snow eats him,
buries him up to the neck.
Another boy, wearing Dad's skates,
falls through the lake ice.

Our arrivals there in time
to surprise Granddad,
home from the bank.
Our faces burn in his whiskers
in the shade of the dark green
shingled house.

Grandma Hattie.
Her kind, dark, deep-set eyes.
Our tummies filled
with her cherry pie.
Gaiety at the little round kid table
by the wood-burning stove.

Our hours of creative play
on the sandy beach.
The sun blazes into blisters.
Bandages, our body armor.
Grandma's tight hugs.
Bursting blisters. More pie.
We race back to the hot shore,
cool waves.

II.

Years pass away.
Our grandparents smile in frames.
Our move back to Dad's family home.
He departs for a year at Princeton.
A Master's in Theology.

Alone with seven kids,
Mom resolves to survive
this sacrifice.

The house eats her grief,
our messy litter
of candy wrappings, toys,
mountains of laundry.
Her heirloom jewelry feeds the vents.
A bag of flour spreads a fine rug.

The lid on an open tuna fish can
almost severs my little brother's toes

as he vaults from the kitchen table
on a dare. Blood. Mayhem.
Curses.

Once the house almost dies
in a violent lightning storm
while Mom is absent.
A fiery bolt sears
the side of the house
next to my big brother's head

Hit by the flu, all of us pale,
wretch. Even the house
spews laundry down the stairs,
stinks of sour milk. Unwashed diapers.

III.

In winter, the hungry house
waits for coal delivery
to the creepy bin in the basement.
When fed, the house shakes
like a beast, choking out smoke
and dust in its hot breath.

In front of the open mouth
of the furnace,
a woman stabs the coals.
Her eyes blaze
as though scathed to the fire.

Mom? I whisper.

Her head snaps around.

"What!!"

Of course, I flee.

My bedroom window opens
a portal onto the lake.
Moonlight splinters
into twisted faces on the walls.
My screams scrape a dance
as the night air echoes
the howls of wolves
when the ice gives way.

IV.

This house still pulls me
to the musty smell
of Granddad's rusty tools
in the garage.
To the kitchen, steaming
with bread and cocoa,
and Grandma Hattie's
flowered cotton apron.

I search for Mother's lost jewels.
Scrub the floors of coal dust.
Collect driftwood for the mantel.

Mom emerges from the house.
"This way", she says. pointing
to the water's edge.
"We can't linger here."

I fear the water.
Dare not venture too far.
"Follow. Follow."

My legs. Heavy as waves.
We sink to the deep
lake bottom of drowned brush.
Twist with the current,
eat the sweet and sour remains
of recollections.

Abandoned: A Haibun

Not far from the dude ranch in Montana. A hike up a path and then a hill overlooking a meadow. I find a decrepit, abandoned cabin. A half-opened door. Stuck in a leaning frame. I push through into a one-room space, half-lit by sunlight sneaking in through gapping slats in the roof and broken shutters. To my left, a rusty bed frame and a stained, sway-backed mattress. A frayed wool blanket, heaped aside. A miserable pillow curved out of shape to fit a head. To the right of the door, a wooden table and one chair, scooted back, against a stove holding a rusty pan and a spoon lodged in a hard mass. On the table, a plate of something crusty, a spoon, and a cup. In disarray. As though the table was pushed away with force

What befell the lonely host—
The mystery of his loss.
No sign of his ghost.

Eilene Toppin Ording

Where Winter Comes Every Year

Among the old photos my family left behind
Are the photos of a snowy life up north.
Even I remember a day when my father
Strung a rope from house to barn so that
When checking on the livestock,
He wouldn't get lost in a whiteout:
The ultimate blizzard event where
The whole world is a white blur of airborne snow.

And looking at these long ago photos of children,
My kin in the snow in front of a log house,
I wonder what they thought
Of cold and snow and blizzards.
Did they shrug and say that it was just January?
Or did someone say, "We ought to move south"?

Did they make the best of it, with sled and snowball
Build a snowman or snow fort, make a snow angel?
Perhaps they grumbled and griped as they
Broke the ice in the water pitcher or
Sawed a hole in the lake to drop a line and fish.

But most of them stayed with Winter--
Stayed to write to California.
Florida. Arizona. Texas.

I can't help but think the ones who stayed
Knew that winter is not unending,

And spring comes sooner than you expect.
For me, home will forever be
Where winter comes every year.

T.K. Pierce

Crying with Strangers

I'm not used to a quiet bar.
A bar where you can hear yourself think.
Nursing my drink,
Taking in the calm. It's foreign.
Performances break the silence.
Raised voices.
Painful memories.
Quiet aches.
I am afraid to share what is in my heart,
Pulling someone else's words to cover it.
Crying with strangers,
    accepting their kindness.
Lost and found.

Dad

I sit in a bar.
Trying not to cry while you read a Christmas story that
    brings so much joy.
There was a time we feared you would never be able to
    do that again.
9 surgeries leaving you a skeleton, hoarse and underfed.

I wept the first time you could really laugh again.
It's hard to imagine now, when you sound so strong.
So I smile while grinch fingers nervously drum,
waiting to come down the mountain again.

Barb's

There is nothing like the sheer joy
    of walking through a second hand book store.
The smell of old books,
Heavy with knowledge and hidden hopes.
Wandering the shelves to search for hidden treasure.
The quiet cheer of finding a book you never
     thought to see.
Money changing hands to leave with a new old friend.

I Don't Have the Words

I don't have the words to tell you how much you mean
to me.
Don't have the words to make you see the person that
I see.
You think that you became no one, like a body adrift
in the sea.
But, you aren't. Not really. Never no one to me.

You are the first person I want to call when life hits an
exciting part.
You are the one who reminds me to stay grounded,
and that I can't do it all.
You are so important, and I don't know how you don't
see it all.

What Things We Do for Love

As I stand behind a bar for the first time in years,
    I reflect.
What things we do for love.

Standing like a fool, praying to make no messes.
Desperate to be a help, not a hindrance.
What things we do for love.

She sits at the bar and keeps handing me money.
She wants to make sure it is fair for you, too.
What things we do for love

They try to help me find things,
Endlessly patient.
What things we do for love.

Coming Home

I sit in amber light, looking out on pieces of my heart.
Away for too long, I didn't know what to expect.
And, like breathing, it all....just....worked.
The heart beat.
The lungs filled.
The love flowed.
Like coming home after a long absence.

Mark Pottorff

Our Ten Acres

I come back to these ten acres,
Not as often as I would like,
To reconnect with my heritage,
The place where I called home,
The land that made me who I am.

I always leave them refreshed, but
Also keenly aware that, while they
Are important to me, they were only
A part of what made me who I am.

Over the years, I have lived in and
Been part of many places, and they
Have all shaped me in different ways
And have become part of who I am.

What I learned years ago is that home
Is not just a piece of land or a house,
Home is those I choose to love, because of
Blood or choice, and they are also
Part of what made me who I am.

The best friend growing up (and his
Entire family); the friend who knows
Me better than most; the woman

Who took me as her own; the two
Children she gave me, and the
Kindred spirits who share their words
And their souls each time we meet,
They have all made me who I am.
They are home.

Dad

I wonder sometimes what you
Would think of me today.
Would you be proud of what
I have made of my life?
Of Patty and the children we have raised?
Of the family we have all become?

In memory I walk with you
Through the west pasture in the
Corner with the pond. We talk
Of your brothers (all gone now)
And of your sisters (only one remains).
You tell me those same stories I
Heard so often as a child; stories
Of Uncle Bob and Walter and Virgil.
Stories that sound brand new each
Time you tell them. We walk through
The gate and go check the cows,
Each one with its own name signifying
The markings on its coat.
We walk through the hay field and marvel
How thick it is this year, even though
We haven't fertilized in a few years.

We walk together until I find
Myself in Grandpa's back forty
All alone, except for your memory.

Mom

I stood in the darkness tonight,
Listening to the tree frogs,
And it took me back, back
To those days so long ago.

To days when you were there,
Calling me back in from the pastures,
Telling me to play one more game,
Urging me to let the dogs alone.

I recall the honks from the horn,
Three long, two short, and then
Home we came. I recall you
And Dee telling us to be careful and
Then hoping we would come back in
One piece. You recognized our youth
But hoped we had the sense to
Live through it and to learn from it.

Those frogs took me back, and
Made me remember, thinking of my
Time with you and all those who
Made me who I am, and
Then I smiled.

Patty

(2024)

She apologizes because she is moving
Slowly or because I may wait a bit for
Her to catch up.

     It seems she has forgotten
The year she spent, watching over me
To ensure I survived.

     Or more perhaps,
She may to have forgotten, "In sickness
And in health, until death do we part."

I doubt either is true, but I still choose
To remind her of both, as I wait, smiling,
Holding the door.

John

By the time I had met you,
You were sixty-four years old,
And I was not your favorite
Person in the world.
I had taken the hand and
Heart of your little girl, and
I was a southern, little bit
Of a redneck, boy from Missouri.

We had a bit of a rough start;
There were shelves I didn't
Want built and perhaps some
Things I should have done better.

But, then, she came along. She
Was my baby girl who came from
Your baby girl, and all was close
To right with the world.

A Place of Rest

We come each Spring to
Clean this small plot
On the hill
Where so much of our
History resides. Just five
Graves are in this chain
Link, but they represent
Shared roots of a much
Larger tree.
We work to preserve this spot,
And tell stories of days gone.
Then, we go our separate
Ways, rejuvenated for another
Year, when we will return
Again to pay our respect for
Those who came before.

Dee

I'm thinking tonight of the lessons
You taught me over the years,
As my other mother and Mom's
Best friend.
Once you've picked it up,
Don't put it down until it's where
It's supposed to be.
Don't talk back, because soap
Tastes like shit.
Love and family
Do not come just from blood.

Haying Season

Seventy miles per hour with the windows down,
The scent of freshly mown hay invades the cab
Of my pickup, bringing back the memories from
So long ago. Four boys without shirts, two girls
In sleeveless t-shirts, an old H Farm-all, and
Grandpa at the wheel, pulling a wagon.
These were our summers, and we worked
To get those 60 pound, square bales into the hayloft,
Never really complaining, because we knew payday
Was coming. When haying season ended, Grandpa
Loaded us all in the back of the pickup and took us
To Estes' drive-in to eat all the burgers, fries, and
Ice cream we wanted. Stuffed to the gills on the drive
Home, we would look forward to next year's feast.

Lake Life

Tree frogs chitter
As a boat goes by
In the distance.
I watch an old western,
And all is at peace
Around me.

A. Rae

Memories of My Childhood

Memories of my childhood,
if I let them stay,
can twist and pull at me,
ache too loud to name.

So I choose to remember
the weekends with you—
where my fragile heart
was never split in two.

We went out to dinner,
you read me every line.
The house was full of laughter,
your time becoming mine.

You called me pumpkin,
had me stir the tea,
said it tasted sweeter
when made with part of me.

You made me wear my coat—
"Sugar melts in rain."
I believed every word,
and felt safe again.

I was never a burden,
only joy, only light.
Your stories took me elsewhere,
out of harm's reach, out of sight.

Away from the absence,
away from neglect,
I was held, I was wanted,
in a home I still protect.

Now you live beyond this world,
your gentle voice is gone.
Your lap, once my shelter,
is something I lean on—

in memory, in quiet,
when the nights fall apart.
Your love lives forever
in the pocket of my heart.

My great-grandma, my great-grandpa,
my truest place to start—
you may be gone from this world,
but never from my heart.

Max, Oh Max

Max, oh Max,
my little calf
his mother turned away,
so no one he had.

My uncle brought you home,
said, He needs a bottle, care.
I volunteered without a pause
abandonment was something I knew how to bear.

I fed you every morning,
every day after school,
again after dinner
that bottle bigger than my hands could hold.

As I watched you grow,
our bond grew just as strong.
After school we played tag,
chasing daylight till it was gone.

We shared apples
from the trees out back.
I'd kiss the tuft upon your head,
then head inside—with one glance back.

Until the day came suddenly
you were big, you were strong.

Out into the pasture you went,
and everything in me felt wrong.

Our daily games were over,
our visits few, far between.
But even now, when I think of you,
I remember what it meant to be seen.

Max, oh Max
Forever my little calf

Another Me's Memories

Some days when the memories keep coming
And the mind has lost control
And I remember all the things
I wish I could forget once and for all

I stop to ponder
About how in another dimension
You were my parents
And I truly felt your love and attention

I think about how that girl
So sweet and innocent must have been
When she wasn't having to deal with
The abuse that came from parental sin

I tried to envision how confident she must be
Never having felt like she wasn't worthy
instead of chaos she had a safe home
One from which she never learned worry

I tried to connect to that girl who knows
What peace in her heart truly feels like
See for myself what a loving home can do
For a little girl who doesn't have to constantly fight

The girl who knows just what it's like to be a kid
And not the kid who raised her sister and brothers

The girl that was tucked in with the book at night
And not the one who is woke up to clean the blood off
    her mother

To be that child whose innocence was protected
Who never feared the night because someone may
    sneak in her room
To be the child who was safe from the dangers of the
    world
To be a child that wasn't groomed

To connect with that sweet child
whose mother never used her as an alibi for adultery
Who never had to step in and defend her little sister
    from abuse
Oh to just glimpse her memories

Memories of catching butterflies
And going to church
Sometimes I feel I'd trade all my memories
Just to connect to hers

She's probably very balanced
Loving and kind
She probably is very naive still
But at least she's not out of her mind

People say my trauma made me stronger
That without it I may be another version of me
That without the trauma I wouldn't have learned

Just how strong I truly can be
To that I say
I get it I do but I'm tired of being strong
I just want to be at peace
I'm tired of getting it all wrong

For my head is a dangerous place
Full of mazes and traps
One wrong turn in it
And instantly I am trapped

Trapped in a memory
From so long ago
That doesn't have any relevance
But into autopilot I go

Allowing my damaged parts
To have control over me
In the moment being consumed by fight or flight
Cortisol pulsing throughout my veins as I struggle
    to breathe

But in another dimension
There's a safe zone I can be
Where in my dreams I visit often
Simply because it's where you raised me

Richard Stimac

Waynesville

During the war, my parents owned a diner
in downtown Waynesville, not far from our trailer.
I remember little, myself being three:
two Sams, one the cook, the other a barber;
pool, pinball. darts, more than a boy could want.
I napped in a closet. My dreams were sweet.
My mom hung a crucifix with palm fronds
above the jukebox. No one noticed it.
That's how it was then, because of the war.
But there was one thing. It was '69,
'70. The diner was the bus stop
from base. They were all draftees, by that time.
In high school, they'd watched on TV the Tet
Offensive my dad fought two years before.
A bus arrived. They disembarked, a cluster
of olive drab fatigues, mesh jungle boots.
Oddly, or not, I remember no faces,
just the waist down, like a photograph cut
in half, as if amputated legs walked
of their own will, torsos, arms, and head gone.
There was one solider, a knife on his belt,
he knelt down, and spoke to me. I liked him.
My mother rushed from behind the register
and whisked me through the glass doors to the counter
and sat me straight on one of the round stools:

"Stay away from them," she said. "They're not good."
I understood she meant, "Not like your father,"
who dropped out of school, married, then enlisted,
all before the nation called the war bad.

Jude MacAllen Tatman

The Gnawing

on cold snow dusted
November mornings,
as the school bus ascended
the long hill out of the valley
i was always wanting
something more perhaps
to climb forever into the sky
before i had ever flown above
to know the truth of rising
into the view of my world
whispered white while wiping
frosted breath away from the cold
window see what we looked like
in the eyes of immortals who dwelt
in heavens observing over old pastures
and desiccated fields defined
by leafless trees of black and gray
limbs peeling bleached boned
along creeks winding down and out
of the hills and hollows with icy water
feeding that big dark river flowing away
to other worlds not yet known.

That gnawing always deep inside
that could make me cry
like my cultural ancestor Huckleberry
who fought with the loathing in his gut
to get away from something
he knew was wrong
or as Tom Sawyer imagined
in daydreams wishing for a world
invented from books read to go
someplace away from it all –

but i was a coward and just looked
out the window of the bus past old barns
peeling in the cold winds of resonant grime
belching out of the dusty cement plant
that loomed over the crumbling once beautiful
neighborhood on the proverbial other side of the
    tracks—
the Southside – where Fulton, Union and Walnut
    streets
climbed the hills to blufftops
trying to escape but it was too late
having been ravaged by years and floods
and poverty beneath a pale of negativity
and dismissiveness that hung in the freezing
air as we trudged into Stowell Elementary
where most of us were led to believe
that it was the only world
we would ever know.

Migration

It's as if the birds never speak to each other; early geese
    fly
south but the mallards quack and splash in the park
    pond.

Do they not know that the sun is starting to grow
    sleepy?
Shouldn't they begin to fly toward warmer days of rest?

Every summer a pair of mourning doves nest in the
    canebrake
beside the house; the dogs anxiously watch their grey
    heads

swivel until frost comes to remind the feathered mates
    of places
where oak trees never lose their leaves remaining alive

through the winter and if the doves start now, they'll
    fly on
to their warm home before December, and if the spring
    is soft

we won't see them much before April. Yet, there are
    these brown
feathered Eurasian Sparrows and Starlings, and Dark-
    Eyed Juncos

crossing the border from Canada— "rats with wings"
dirty dark pigmented invaders won't return to from
      where they came,

shit all over everything. They'd rather stay here in the
      cold outside,
begging at birdfeeders and stealing food from the
      mouths

of beautiful Great American songbirds who have
      always lived here—
Cardinals, Chickadees, Bluebirds, Buntings, Jays,
      Warblers, and Tufted Titmice

whose beauty beyond the window in winter provides
      entertainment for humans
and house cats alike, shortly after the pods of the
      milkweeds have opened

casting seeds to the winds. If only those lazy birds
      knew how to gather
and store those seeds, the birdfeeder industry, as
      well as

the Ornithological Control Enforcement Agency,
would become obsolete.

The Dead

The dead do not think
of what happened
to their souls that sleep
only in the stories
and histories of the living
left behind.

The dead don't remember
time; it stopped when
they died, no need
to watch the clock
any longer as it steals
their life away.

The dead care not
of what or who remains,
being severed from
any sense of property,
loyalty or love.

The dead have no memories,
all their thoughts and plans
are lost to once lucid dreams
that will never be
dreamt again.

The dead are gone,
from where they fell, gone
from the suffering, gone
from concern, gone –
free from shackles
of commitment, elation,
remorse, shame, sorrow.

The dead no longer
have reason to remember
birthdays, anniversaries,
social security numbers,
passwords or in which drawer
were kept the good scissors.

Yet the billions of dead
from prehistory until now,
once knew – from their birth day
to the last day – this one thing;
somehow, it is still better
to be alive.

Blizzard in Spring

i have lived long enough to know
that in dimming afternoons
of blowing snows, to call the horses
to the stables, while the cows are many,
sturdy strong and able to fend for themselves
forming huddles their white faces leeward
head-to-head, shoulder to shoulder, black rumps
clenched like onyx bulwarks holding back
the pale windy tide, hooves drearily dug in
the mire of manure and mud they forlornly brace
for a freezing late winter whiteout whistling
from somewhere beyond the dark naked trees
on the ridge, over pastures pale silent,
the blizzard blows heavier covering
recently sprouted tender leaves of grass.
Yet still –

some calves are lost to killing frosts
no matter what is done they will not see
the hopeful warmth of dawn on easy summer days,
to romp and play among the herd, but instead they lie
dead trammeled along the barbed wire fence
by frantic youthful routes toward the hope
of escape from the white turning black echo.

And so, i know what happens when life is conceded
inevitably to attend more funerals than christenings
and first communions, when the days are scattered
like petals blown away across the open fields in May
where we walked barefoot on the warm days, but all
is soon gone, leaving holes dug deep in the cold
Missoura clay where grief is thrown into a void
once filled with precious memories, still so clear
after all these years, yet so far behind
to become only ghosts of emotions
to haunt on occasions when i feel
it is permissible to cry.

Annie Hall

Yesterday,
for the first time
in forty-eight years,
I awakened to learn
that my first serious fantastical
infatuation was no longer attainable –
except on digitized celluloid
when watched transports
this awkward *acne vulgaris* afflicted
adolescent Hannibal High School
student of semi-shy mediocrity
      – nervously on
        perhaps his second
        or third driving date –
back to that singular Saturday night
in Quincy Illinois at *The Adams Cinema*,
holding a girl's hand in the flickering
darkness, then, and still today,
I wish had been yours,
Ms. Keaton.
I really loved your hat.

Compliment

"You look like Michael McDonald"
said she of an indeterminate age; vintage, like me.
Well, I'll take that as a compliment I said, red-faced,
     smiling.

"and you sound like him, too! Do you sing?"
Yes, but never able to hit his chorus of high notes;
"Who can?" she stated in light retort.

Exiting the clinic, where we vintage folk
go for weekly or biweekly maintenance,
we disappeared, our encounter perhaps

lost forever in a small sea of autos—
It's the hair, I thought, sitting in my vintage
Jeep, *and the tortoiseshell Ray Bans,* hiding

vintage eyes, although I am younger
than the Doobie Brother by nearly a decade,
but it's not the model year; it's always the mileage.

Driving through town I tell Siri to pull up
Minute by Minute, windows down music blasting,
late September sun warming my face, cool winds

in my hair, my *Olukai* sandaled foot on the gas,
     excitedly

looking forward to telling my wife and friends of the
    encounter
and compliment, looking forward to this week's karaoke
    night at the pub —

oh, what a fool believes.

Agnes Vojta

Vineyard in Dresden

The path between the ivied walls
is paved in sandstone. Grass
grows from the cracks. I follow
the trails of childhood.

The cobwebbed door
has not been opened in a long time,
but someone cleared the steps
leading to it. I climb

the stairs into the vineyards,
breathe history, mine and the land's.
Lush and green, the grapes
promise a rich harvest.

Below, the river sings a love song
to the city that is no longer mine.
Eighteen years change
a person and a place.

Not even the trees
are the same; the drought
felled the old oak in the clearing
we called the witches' dance hall.

But the hills and the river
are still there, and dearer
to me than the castles
and cathedrals that lure the tourists.

And the summer light
through the maples remains
unchanged, as all else
grows old and distant.

Flotsam

I shipped my past to this continent
in a box I open rarely. In it,

my mother's amber necklace
and my grandmother's silver cross,

a dried flower from my prom bouquet,
ribboned letters from old lovers,

notebooks with poems written
thirty years ago in another tongue,

a leather pouch I carried around my neck,
a brass key that opens no lock I know,

a photograph of the house on the hill
that stands now empty,

where my voice still echoes, unheard,
five thousand miles away.

We Call It Gravity

Each summer, I return. I open
the gate and climb the stairs
through the garden to the house.

My steps quicken. I feel the jolt
of coming home, like a comet
that gains momentum as it races

closer. Even at its aphelion,
the comet never loses the memory
of the star, and the star does not release

the comet from its stenciled ellipse.
Why? We call it gravity but cannot
explain why it exists or how it works.

Gravity. Or love.

Rewired

In mom's kitchen, Grandma's
measuring cup is still
on the shelf, her nutmeg grater
hangs from its hook.

For sugar and salt, we still use
the little wooden shovels.
I set the table
with the familiar

blue-and-white dishes,
the placemats my sister
and I weaved that Christmas
we got the looms.

In the pantry, I still reach
for the light switch on the left
where it no longer is.
Dad rewired the kitchen

twenty years ago. I cannot
rewire my brain, cannot train
my hand to reach
to the other side.

Naming

My first day here it snowed,
and birds like drops of blood
sat in the grey-green branches of a tree.
I was a stranger. Did not know
the names of tree or birds.

Naming is knowing.
Naming means: to tell apart,
to be familiar with the detail
that separates one from the other.
Familiarity breeds love.

I learned to name the cedars
and the cardinals, anemone
and great blue heron, spiderwort
and wild geranium. Every year,

I add new names: white avens,
thimbleweed, rose-breasted grosbeak –
every one another root
I grow here.

First Christmas in Missouri

I miss the carols. The boys' choir
singing Bach's Christmas oratorio.

Mom's collection of wooden nutcrackers.
The fat little angels with their green wings.

Christmas pyramids and Herrnhut paper stars.
Mulled wine at the Christkindl market.

I find Lebkuchen at Aldi.
Imported from Germany.

I do not like Lebkuchen.
But they smell of cinnamon, anise,

and home. That winter, we are eating
Lebkuchen well into March.

A Fractal of Generations

The conifers are taller than the house now.
Whoever planted them did not think
far enough into the future.

I scan my mother's face, search for signs
that should concern me. Quake
at the thought of seeing her changed.

My doll house is still in the attic.
The dolls are lost.
I did not pass them to my daughter.

I see my future in my mother's feet –
the deformed toe joints,
no longer flexible, are my heirloom.

Each spring, mom buys an aquatic plant.
Its floating leaves give birth to miniature copies
of themselves, a fractal of generations.

My mother's hands no longer play the piano.
Sheet music wilts on the shelves.
I hallucinate the sound of sisterly duets.

The Yew Trees with Their Bitter Berries

The house sleeps
behind curtains of wine leaves.
The black-and-white tiles
lay crooked and cracked
on overgrown paths.

I see, once a year,
my parents' faces
as in a flip book
that makes time visible
and foreshadows endings.

The garden dozes
in the deep dark green
of rhododendrons
and of the yew trees
with their bitter berries.

To Call this Place Home

Triangular patterns of light and shadow on the water. A dragonfly lands on my kayak, stares at me with bulging green eyes, does not move its translucent wings with the black spots. In Chinese culture, dragonflies symbolize change and instability. I want neither.

Next week, I will travel home to see my mother. I will climb the hill and walk through the garden with the old rhododendrons as I have a thousand times. Familiar smells, familiar sights. But Dad won't be there. I wish I were not burdened with the forethought of further grief. I steer my boat through the water willows onto the bank. Low-hanging branches brush against my shoulders, greenbriar snags my pants as I follow the faint trace up the hill to the old homestead.

Only the chimney still stands, its fieldstone masonry overgrown with vines. Glistening quartz veins adorn the rocks that form the mantel. Nothing else remains of the family who came here to live their dream. Who called this place home.

The One who Left

Like water flowing downhill,
letters now travel
only in one direction.

Life goes on for those who stayed;
a circle with one person missing
is still a circle.

The one who left floats,
fragile tethers frayed
by the teeth of time and distance.

After some years,
even the Christmas cards
remain unanswered.

Cam Whelr MD

On The Cusp

                    of entering my 60th year, I was
preparing to join friends for an event when menopausal
flashes of heat-rage & panic overwhelmed me. All at
once, I was falling fast & deep as Marvel Cave into
shame-storms where all my grannies & aunties &
the random churchy women I've known kept whirl-
winding their habitual judgements inside my blame-
chambered mind. And I found myself entirely paralyzed
about what to wear & bile surged up my throat, as I
kept telling myself, *Not one person will even notice.*
But still, I went on kicking myself purple, while fully
knowing I should've long ago outgrown these cyclic
self-bludgeoning impulses. In the end, I just threw
something on & attended the swearing in of my friend
as Poet Laureate of this very red state we both inhabit.

This younger brother poet, with his farm-boy vibe
reminds me of all the guys I grew up with, all the small-
town-Joes who never wanted me to be anything at all to
them. And when he takes the stage in his plaid jacket,
hat & boots to read "Flyover Country," his words perform
alchemy, become solid, sure machinery for stamping
empathy into human hearts. And my breath catches
as he swears his oath to uphold *The Constitution of
the United States of America* — not The Constitution

of our very middle-of-the-middle state — but
THE CONSTITUTION whose foundations are so
attacked & disregarded these days. And I know beyond
knowing this poet brother will uphold his oath with
greater vigor & reverence than POTUS, SCOTUS,
cabinet or congress. And this good knowing grips my
chest without warning & I am tearfully in touch with
the terror I've been carrying in my belly every day.

And just like that, his rise to Laureate for some
unknown reason also heals me a bit somewhere deep
down in my Ozarkian girlhood. And for the first time
in what seems like an epoch, I feel something new
welling in me. It makes no sense that I feel suddenly,
palpably hopeful. No sense in the midst of this our
present peril, to be absurdly assured that some deep
connection will twine & bind between us & all y'all
as we struggle toward expressing the ineffable. No
sense at all to know at depth someHow, someWhere,
someWhen — no matter how far off they seem to us
now — someOne will weather these days in kind &
generous togethering, until Time ripens enough once
again to nourish & rebuild humanity anew.

Clarence Wolfshohl

Bluebonnet Spring

The first week bluebonnet
is seed to old pictures–
my father leading me by the hand
in a field of ocean blue
above the still brown pasture.
Clustered around the crumbling well,
once death pit for our mare's colt
that old cowboy Travis went down to get,
the flowers trampled to the ground
by the mare's vigilance and our resurrecting.

Years later in mid-March
on rare homecomings
I went with my father into the blue fields
to pick the same bouquets
we always took to the family graves,
and I remembered the colt's broken red body
and my father's silence.
I don't know if he always remembered,
but the first bluebonnets caused him
to walk the higher field in late afternoon
and wait for the ocean of blue
that always comes.

Spring Blooms

Along the Llano and San Saba,
the bluebonnets bloom
followed soon in their blue glory
by Indian paintbrush's layers of red.

But the verbena is always first,
hugging the earth like spots
of purple moss, the first
signs of spring among the hills.

I remember those colors
when here above the Missouri
I see the delicate petals
of the white spring beauty

streaked with pink and rose,
blushing in their nakedness
in the sun after the ice
of winter has unshackled the loam.

The Wisteria

A decade, maybe two, ago
in this remote corner pocket of nine acres
beside an old cedar, tatters like skirts
of a nun, I planted the cutting.

It caught on despite my doubts
and was twisted about dying limbs
within a couple of years. And I guess
each year it went higher and its tendrils

reached wider and absorbed the cedar
into its heart, but, as I said, this spot
is remote and the other trees and brush
grew, also, and I did not notice

until now. And there it is this spring day,
a full tree of its own, royal with blooms.

Locating Redbuds on Red Bud Lane

They line the road hemmed by cliffs
each side as it climbs east from Crow's Fork,
but on the hill they disappear
as if the effort is too great.
That royal exhibit leaves you
wanting more, so you turn onto
our lane—lure of nomenclature—
and just before you give up,
no redbuds in sight among
the still grey branches, there they
are tumbling down the hawk draw.

Wolf Tree

It stands alone on the last bend
of the road before I'm home.
Its limbs spread fifty feet
from the massive trunk, burled
grotesque from broken limbs,
its crown broad and flat.

Yards away is the wall of the woods;
the wolf oak's millions of siblings
stretch miles toward Missouri
bottomland. They spire upward, limbs
turned skyward toward the sun.
They grow straight, no blemish
of burl nor gnarl of wind.

When I split their wood against winter cold,
the grain is long and my maul cleaves
the logs with ease, but the wolf
turns my ax and maul into toys
that bounce off or get trapped
in its sinews. The wolf howls defiance.

Fishing at Lake of the Ozarks

Voices drift over the water,
phrases of the minutiae of the craft—
temperature, depth of water,
glitter of a novice's cast.

The waves glint and open
holes in the water to let
out the sun that plays
in shimmers under our cap-bills.

The celluloid lights dance
with our gaze and blind
us momentarily in the morning
shush of water and wind

until a fish strikes, pulls
the line taut, the nylon
catching a lightning bolt's
surprise parallel to the water.

I reel in the fish and lift it
into luminescence, unhook
it, and re-bait the barb,
a smear of minnow-shine on my hand.

The Piscine Y

This morning at the Y
my vision filled with piscine life
as if we were all in an aquarium
or riding the current of some
creek, river, or sea.

Walkers rounded the track
like goldfish in a bowl
with nowhere to go
except in circles. Most in slow
but consciously paced stride
kept to the outside
glancing at the walls as if they
were glass, and beyond, a strange dry day.

Among the iron, sharks muscled their weight
with grunts and narrow-eyed concentration—
the body builders hard as hammerheads,
studious of their skill as great whites. But loud
as sun perch leaping into sparkles
on a roaring day.

                    Young women sashayed
among treadmills, rowers, and walkers
adorned like fantails and glowing like neon tetra.
They darted their eyes toward the splash and laugh
of the sharks, but kept within the coral tangle
of exercise machines, shy of the sharks' razor teeth.

And then there were we old clowns
fish, going through motions to keep
alive, thinking about the pastries
we'd rather be eating or the loungers
we'd rather be reclining in, and rehearsing
the same old self-deprecating lines
about waking up, this fine morning
still breathing or wondering why
the stationary bicycles never get us
to our destination.

O, Pioneer: Our House

Our house was the first frame home
on our twist of a road in these woods.
Four log houses started this community
on Red Bud, spelled as two words
by the old Dutchman who made
the first road sign of cedar's red heart.
Not logs hewn from the miles of white oak
that surround us, but from kits
with each log numbered like a giant
doll house, some assembly required.
Two other frames started a month or two
afterwards, but this one—ours—was the pioneer.

None of the log houses are occupied
by the original families—death, divorce, age.
We built a frame house because I knew how
after many summers turning brown
as a berry on the concrete-slab prairies
of construction boom San Antonio.
So Patricia sighted walls and plumbed
corners while I used pulleys and ropes
and the surrounding trees to muscle
two-by skeletons straight and true.
All three of the frame houses are still occupied
by the original families although smaller—
death, divorce, age.

I awoke this morning dreaming
of our pioneer days building
this house, this community,
our white smiles all over
our brown berry faces,
and Patricia's eye squinting
along a top plate that had no ending.

The Ghosts of Toledo

(Toledo, Callaway County, Missouri)

I walked down the shaded slope
across Craighead Branch east
into Toledo, to the crossroads
where two gravel and two paved roads
meet, charting how the county
judges our neck of the woods.

A few rock foundations are scattered
through the woods, filled with brush
or third growth oaks. They crumble
around the roots, whisper chorus
to the squawks of jays.

The old school house releases birds
from windows and roof holes,
where legend says Jesse James
hid and taught among veteran
guerillas in the village of two hundred.

Only the old Unity Church
with its churchyard of stones
and decaying crosses dating back
to the 1840s still stands.
Even a house across from the church
on the crossroads, built
after I first walked these woods,
now composts with those older ghosts.

At night owls moan among the oaks
and fox scream like women in pain
down the hollows in mating season.
As I walk home, the sun sinks behind
far ridges, the darkening shades
of purple before me joining the hum

Clay

I've worked my garden for thirty years,
built rich soil on the slab of clay
like the islanders of Inishmore
who composted seaweed into soil
over centuries; but at bottom
it is potter's clay—the color
of terra cotta. I know a creek bank
with streaks of grey and a red as bright
as jetting blood, squeezed finger thin
by the meters-high moraine when ice
capped us here before seeds breathed.

The Poets:

Keely Alexander is a licensed psychologist, professor, and enthusiastic cat mom with a deep passion for understanding the human experience. Through writing, she explores themes of resilience, connection, and self-discovery, using poetry as a means to process, reflect, and engage with the world. Whether in the classroom, the therapy room, or on the page, she remains committed to caring and showing up for herself and others with compassion and authenticity.

Walter Bargen was the first Poet Laureate for the State of Missouri. Born in the shadow of the 82nd Airborne, he discovered jumping out of a tree in a nearby swamp only results in fracturing a left arm (when he was too young to know better) but it didn't stop him from exploring the world of words. He has published 29 books of poems. His latest is *Orwell at the Kremlin*.

John A. Clayton is a longtime resident of Maries County, Missouri, where he lives in the woods. He has worked as a wood cutter, logger, construction worker, lineman, soldier, school teacher, water tower painter, lawyer, judge and gardener. John has been published in *Gasconade Review, Wine Drunk Sidewalk: Ship Wrecked in Trumpland, Rye Whiskey Review and Reported For Duty*. He was Poet Laureate for Belle, Missouri during COVID.

Jon Freeland is a poet and performer who lives in Jefferson City with his wife, Joanna, and son, Alistair. He started the Gumbo Bottoms Open Mic in

December 2019 with owner Steve Erangey and arts community coordinator Suzanne Luther. After having to pause the open mic in 2020 due to COVID-19, he restarted it as a monthly gathering in September 2021. It has continued ever since, beginning with a small group of dedicated poets and growing to include features from all over the country including New York, Indiana, Ohio, Kansas, Texas, and Florida thanks to strong friendships with the Osage Arts Community, Columbia Writers Guild, and poetry ambassadors in Rolla and St. Louis. It is these deep human connections, the love and respect that our regulars have for each other, and Steve's vision combined with Allen Tatman's genius that has fashioned the Gumbo Bottoms Single Pot Still Poets Society (or GBSPSPS, if you're trying to call your cat), meeting the first Monday of the month at 7p except when holidays or special features push the date back.

Ken Gierke is retired and has lived in Missouri since moving from Western New York in 2012. A Pushcart Prize nominee, his writing has appeared as two micro-chapbooks from *Origami Poems Project* and in numerous anthologies, including *River Dog Zine* and the *Gasconade Review.* His poetry collections, *Glass Awash* in 2022, *Heron Spirit* in 2024, and *Random Riffs* in 2025, were published by Spartan Press. His website: https://rivrvlogr.com/

Janelle Harris is a lifelong artist, painter, and creative spirit who finds inspiration in the nature, travel, and diverse cultures. She is a proud mom to humans and dogs, an avid baker, and a lover of food, and friend to many.

Melinda Hemmelgarn is a Registered Dietitian who appreciates the power of food and words. She hosts *Food Sleuth Radio* on KOPN (89.5) in Columbia, MO, and writes poetry to promote social and environmental justice.

Julianne King is a mother and poet currently splitting her life between the United States and Mexico after the eight-month detention and eventual deportation of her partner. The increasing danger to their Mexican-American twins forced the family to separate. With four of her children, her family, and her...Chris left behind, King continues to write her way out of the trauma. King's works have appeared in *Dreaming Towards Liberation,* and the *South Florida Poetry Journal.* She has also published five chapbooks including her most recent *The Fall of a Nation* on Live.

Caitlin Korte is a nonprofit compliance officer who carries home in fragments: shared laughter, difficult moments, and enduring love for family and friends. Her writing explores the spaces where daily life and human connection intersect, capturing what it means to belong.

Barbara Harris Leonhard is the author of *Three-Penny Memories: A Poetic Memoir* (2022) and *The Lost Book of Zeroth (2025). She is co-author of Too Much Fun to Be Legal* (2024) and *Broken Rengay: Unruly Poetry* (2025). She's a Pushcart Prize and Best of the Net nominee. Trending Poets named her Poet of the Year in 2023 and 2024. Her poetry has been translated into Italian, Albanian, and Chinese. She is the editor for *MasticadoresUSA* and *FEED THE HOLY.* Her WordPress blog is *Extraordinary Sunshine Weaver.*

A Minnesota native now living in Missouri, **Eilene Toppin Ording** is the daughter of a family of writers, teachers and farmers. Among her interests are history, Celtic culture and genealogy.

T.K. Pierce is a poet and performer from Missouri. Her emotion-centered style is characterized by its brevity and focus on making sense of the world around her. Pierce often writes in the moment, getting struck by inspiration and needing to get it out of her head and onto a page right then. She has been part of the Gumbo Bottoms Single Pot Still Poets Society since 2022, and enjoys reading, embroidery, video games, and bad puns.

Mark Pottorff is a retired public educator, who taught H.S. English for ten years before going over to the dark side to become an administrator. Two constants in his life have been family and poetry, and the former is heavily reflected in the latter. His free verse poetry often embodies the human battle between the need to express and release our tenderest moments and the societal pressure to keep it all in as we process the trauma of our lives. Mark has poems in the Gumbo Bottoms Single Pot Still Poets Society's anthology, *A Drop of the Pure* (2025) and has published his first book of poems, *Around That Old Table* (2026), both from Spartan Press.

A. Rae is a poet, painter, wife, mother, and dedicated community advocate. A survivor who channels her personal healing journey into her art, she uses poetry and visual expression as tools for transformation and growth. Her work guides readers through the process of acknowledging pain, transmuting it into strength, and ultimately arriving at healing. Beyond her creative practice, A. Rae founded a mobile soup kitchen serving homeless, homebound, and low-income individuals in her community. She also manages a local community art gallery and actively supports organizations working to advance justice for marginalized communities across America.

Richard Stimac lives in the St. Louis, Missouri (USA) area. He has published two poetry books: *Blood, Water, and Stone* (Spartan Press, 2026); and *Bricolage* (Spartan Press, 2022). Richard explores time and memory through the landscape and humanscape of the St. Louis region. He invites you to follow his poetry Facebook page: "Richard Stimac poet".

Jude MacAllen Tatman is a Missouri poet, historian, author, and publican, born in Hannibal and raised on the family homestead along the west bank of the Mississippi River. He received his BA in History, with an English minor, from Northwest Missouri State University, and earned his MFA in Creative Writing with the University of Nebraska at Omaha's Writers Workshop. Past vocations include work as a farmhand, union Ironworker's hand (Local 577, Burlington, Iowa), deckhand on towboats on the Mississippi and Ohio rivers, pizza delivery driver while also a semi-pro baseball player in West Texas, waiter and bartender, corporate sales and marketing, and an archivist/historian for Missouri State Parks. He also lost on Jeopardy. MacAllen and his wife, Marilee, own and operate Paddy Malone's Irish Pub in Jefferson City, where they live with a brace of bird dogs on a bluff overlooking the Missouri River in a century-old bungalow that belongs to a couple of somewhat ornery cats.

Agnes Vojta grew up in Germany and now lives in Rolla, Missouri where she teaches physics at Missouri S&T and hikes the Ozarks. She is the author of *Porous Land*, *The Eden of Perhaps*, *and A Coracle for Dreams* (Spartan Press), and her fourth collection *Love Song to Gravity* has come out from Stubborn Mule Press in 2025. Agnes is associate editor of *Thimble Literary Magazine* and host of the Poetry at the Pub reading series in Rolla. Her poems have appeared in a variety of magazines; you can read some of them on her website agnesvojta.com.

Cam Whelr, MD is a dis/Abled pediatrician, poet, writer and visual artist whose words appear in *Pleiades*, *The Rumpus*, *Ice Floe* and *Collaborature*, among other journals and anthologies. She is a Best of The Net & Pushcart nominee whose works explore trauma-forged & chronically ill embodiment. She forages & cultivates a deeply nourished life through creative practices by staying well-rooted in a[r]tivist & res[t] sistance communities from mid-Missouri where two affable service dogs allow her to share their home. She can be found as @CamWhelr on IG, FB, BSky, and at Substack: Lucent Splinter.

Clarence Wolfshohl, professor emeritus at William Woods University, has been active in the small press as writer and publisher for over fifty years, publishing poetry and non-fiction in many journals, both print and online, including *North Dakota Quarterly*, *Concho River Review*, *San Pedro River Review*, *Agave*, *Green Hills Literary Lantern*, *Cape Rock*, *New Letters*, *Southwestern American Review*, *Gasconade Review*, *Home Planet News*, and *The Mailer Review*. Among his recent publications are the e-chapbook *Scattering Ashes* (Virtual Artists

Collective, 2016), the chapbooks *Holy Toledo* (El Grito del Lobo Press, 2017), *Queries and Wonderments* (El Grito del Lobo Press, 2017), *Armadillos & Groundhogs* (2019), *Scattering Ashes* (El Grito del Lobo, 2025), and his collection *Play-Like* (Alien Buddha Press, 2025). He has been nominated for a Pushcart Prize twice. Wolfshohl lives in the suburbs of Toledo, Missouri, with his two cats.

This project was made possible, in part, by generous support from the Osage Arts Community.

Osage Arts Community provides temporary time, space and support for the creation of new artistic works in a retreat format, serving creative people of all kinds — visual artists, composers, poets, fiction and nonfiction writers. Located on a 152-acre farm in an isolated rural mountainside setting in Central Missouri and bordered by ¾ of a mile of the Gasconade River, OAC provides residencies to those working alone, as well as welcoming collaborative teams, offering living space and workspace in a country environment to emerging and mid-career artists. For more information, visit us at www.osageac.org